Paul
the Missionary

IVA JEWEL TUCKER • ILLUSTRATED BY **RON HESTER**

BROADMAN PRESS
Nashville, Tennessee

Dewey Decimal Classification: J 225.92
Subject heading: PAUL, APOSTLE
Printed in the United States of America

Contents

Saul of Tarsus

"I'm going down to the harbor, Father," said young Saul. "I won't be gone long."

The active boy liked to be outdoors. He sat on the big ropes on the wharf, watching the workers unload the ships. The sights and smells and sounds of the harbor meant fun to Saul.

Saul lived in Tarsus in Cilicia. He was proud to be a Jew, proud of the traditions of his mother and father. The boy listened carefully to the stories his mother told him about his family. Saul liked for her to remind him that he had been named for the first king of Israel. Every sabbath day in this Jewish home, Saul's father read from the sacred scrolls. Saul learned the verses that all the Jewish boys knew. He was obedient to the Jewish laws.

Sometimes Saul worked at the loom in his father's shop, throwing the shuttle back and forth across the threads. His father had taught him how to weave the cloth which they made from the skin of goats. Boy Saul liked to read and study and write, but he was glad his father was teaching him the art of tentmaking. He knew that every good Jewish father taught his trade to his sons.

"I saw some soldiers near the wharf today, Father. I was a little scared."

"They won't hurt us, Saul. They are Roman soldiers, sent here because Tarsus is part of the Roman Empire. The soldiers help guard our city. We are Roman citizens, Son."

"I'm proud to be a Roman citizen, Father. Today some of the boys called me Paul, my Roman name. I like it. I'm glad to be a Jew, too." Saul felt good inside.

Later, Saul went to Jerusalem to study. He wanted to become a rabbi, a leader of the Jews. Saul kept hearing about a person named Stephen. Stephen was a Jew like Saul, but Stephen had joined Jesus' followers and had accepted Christ as his Savior. Jesus had already been crucified. But he had risen from the dead and had talked with his disciples before he went on to heaven.

The followers of Jesus knew that he was the Son of God, the Messiah they had waited for so long. The faithful disciples kept on preaching and healing the sick. To help the disciples, seven special workers were chosen. Stephen was one of these. Stephen gave money to the poor and preached about the love of Jesus. But Saul felt that Stephen was all wrong.

"Jesus of Nazareth!" Saul said. "How can Stephen preach that Jesus was the Messiah? Surely Stephen knows that Jesus was tried in court and then crucified. How could someone who died in disgrace like that be the Messiah?"

9

Some of the Jewish leaders were angry at
Stephen. They got people to say untrue things
about him, and Stephen was arrested. In the
court, someone said: "This person has been
saying bad things about the Temple and about
God's law."

The high priest turned to Stephen. "Is this
true?"

Stephen told the men of the council that
they had killed the Savior when they crucified
Jesus. "You are heathen in heart and heathen

10

in hearing. You have betrayed and murdered
the Messiah!"

The judges were furious. They screamed at
Stephen and put their hands over their ears so
they could not hear what he was saying. Then
the men of the court jumped up and grabbed
Stephen and dragged him outside the walls of
the city. There they yelled and began throwing
rocks at Stephen. The men got madder and
madder. They took off their outer robes so
they could throw bigger stones.

The robes were placed in front of a man who stood watching. He was thinking: "Stephen preached bad things, so of course he deserves to die." The dignified young man folded him arms and looked on calmly as the stones gashed into Stephen.

Just then a big rock struck Stephen on the head and blood gushed out. He fell to the ground. As Stephen died he prayed out loud: "Lord Jesus, forgive them for this sin."

The man who stood watching was Saul of Tarsus.

Thinkback: What was the trade of Saul's father?

Why did Saul think Stephen was wrong?

The Great Change

After Stephen's murder, Saul hated the Christians more than ever. He went into homes and arrested women as well as men, locking them all in jail. But Jesus' friends kept on telling the good news. Even when they had to leave town to keep Saul from finding them, they talked about Jesus. Many persons heard and believed that Jesus really was the Messiah.

"Write some letters for me," Saul asked the high priest in Jerusalem. "Ask the leaders in Damascus to help me find all the disciples. I will arrest them and bring them back in chains!"

The high priest wrote the letters, and Saul left at once for Damascus. "Just wait till I get hold of those Jesus people," Saul must have said. "How can they believe all those lies!"

Saul was so mad he could hardly wait to fasten the chains around the arms and legs of the believers.

It was about the middle of the day. Saul and his friends were hurrying toward Damascus. Saul held the letters which were going to help him catch Jesus' disciples. Suddenly a bright light flashed on Saul. He was so frightened he threw himself down on the road.

A voice spoke in the Hebrew language: "Saul, Saul, why do you persecute me? You are only hurting yourself."

Saul was too afraid to look up. He asked weakly, "Who are you?"

"I am Jesus, the one you are persecuting. Stand up!"

Saul got to his knees. He opened his eyes and tried to look up, but the light was too bright. Saul stood up and covered his eyes with his hands.

"What do you want me to do?"

The voice of Jesus said: "Saul, go to Damascus. There you will be told what to do next."

Saul opened his eyes but could not see anything. The men who were with Saul led him on to Damascus.

For three days Saul could not see. He did not eat or drink anything for those three days. Then a good man named Ananias came to see Saul. The Lord had told Ananias to go to Saul and touch him so that he could see again. Ananias didn't want to do this. He knew that Saul had been mistreating the Christians all over Jerusalem. And he had heard that Saul was here in Damascus to make more arrests. But Ananias did as God told him, and Saul's sight came back.

How happy Saul was! He was glad he could see again. Most of all he was glad he had met Jesus, the Christ. Saul knew that Jesus was his Savior, and Saul was baptized right there in Damascus.

Thinkback: Why was Saul going to Damascus? What happened to Saul on the road to Damascus?

17

Escape in the Night

The town of Damascus was dark, but the moon was shining brightly. Saul was talking to God. He was not afraid, but he knew that his enemies in Damascus wanted to kill him. Saul wanted to go back to Jerusalem, but there was no way for him to get out of Damascus. The city gates were carefully guarded day and night.

Saul's life was in danger because he had been preaching about Jesus. He had been telling everyone that Jesus who had been crucified was actually the Son of God. Some of the people Saul talked to believed in Jesus. A little group of these Christians were in the room where Saul was praying. They had been praying, too, but they tiptoed to the side of the room to talk. Saul kept on praying.

"I'm afraid," one of the young men whispered. "I know the enemies are looking everywhere for Saul. They're going to kill him if we don't think of a way he can get out of Damascus."

"What can we do? The city gates are watched every minute — there's just no way for Saul to escape."

Another Christian spoke up: "I have an idea. It's dangerous, but it might work. The enemies are guarding the city gates, but they aren't watching the wall. How about helping Saul escape over the wall?"

The friends decided to help Saul make this daring escape from the city. They made a large, strong basket and tied ropes to the sides. Saul and the men walked quietly through the dark streets of Damascus. Their only light was the light of the moon. When they got to a friend's house which was by the city wall, they climbed to the roof. Saul got in the basket. His friends lifted the basket over the wall.

20

Using the ropes, the men let the basket slowly down the other side of the wall. As soon as the basket touched the ground, Saul slipped out quietly. Moving in the shadows so the enemy would not see him, Saul started on his trip back to Jersualem.

Thinkback: How did Saul's friends help him escape from Damascus?

21

Man with a Mission

What a change! Saul of Tarsus became stronger in his work for Christ than he had been in persecuting the believers. The Jewish leaders no longer liked Saul. Some of the followers of Jesus did not trust him, either. A group of Jesus' friends were in a home, talking about Saul.

"This man Saul is a beast. I don't like him. This is probably a trick to catch us all."

A disciple named Barnabas walked to the front of the room. He was big and strong and

23

a firm believer. The men and women all looked up to Barnabas.

"I like Saul," Barnabas said. "If you had heard the good preaching Saul did in Damascus, you would like him, too. Forgive him. He is a Christian now. He is sorry he did those bad things."

The people were surprised to hear what Barnabas said, but they believed him. At last they knew that Saul was their friend, a follower of Jesus.

When the church at Antioch asked Barnabas and Saul to go as their missionaries, they all prayed about it. They knew that people everywhere needed to know the good news of the Messiah, the risen Lord. The Christians walked with Barnabas and Saul to the harbor where they got on a big ship. Saul was thrilled to be going on this important journey—his first missionary trip. The two men sailed from Antioch to an island named Cyprus. With them went a young helper, John Mark.

In Cyprus, Saul started using his Roman name, Paul. He and Barnabas preached and taught and prayed and talked about Jesus.

When the boat docked near a town, Paul and Barnabas could hardly wait to jump to the shore and meet the people.

The missionaries went from Cyprus to the mainland. One day John Mark decided that he did not want to go any farther. Maybe the missionary trip was not as exciting as he thought it was going to be. So he quit and went back home. Paul was upset at first, but later he forgave the young friend.

Everywhere he went, Paul had a sense of mission. He had a goal — an important purpose to work toward. Paul's mission was to serve God. When Paul met Jesus on the Damascus road, his life turned all the way around. He made up his mind to tell every person he met about Jesus Christ. Saul the persecutor had become Paul the apostle.

Thinkback: Who was the disciple who stood up for Paul when Jesus' followers did not believe he had really changed?

In what city was the church which sent out Barnabas and Paul as missionaries?

What was Paul's mission?

Suffering for Jesus

Paul and Barnabas continued on their
missionary journey. They traveled to Lystra
and Derbe and other cities, preaching the
good news. In Lystra, a crippled man sat
listening to Paul. The man had never walked.
When he heard Paul tell about Jesus, the man
had faith that God could heal him.

"Stand up!" said Paul. The man who had
never taken a step got to his feet and walked.

"I just can't believe it," said a girl who was watching. "That man's crippled feet have always been bent back. Now he is walking toward Paul!"

"Oh, Paul is great," a man said. "He must be some sort of god."

Paul spoke up at once: "No, we are not gods. We are human beings just like you. We bring you news of Jesus, your Savior. Trust Jesus, not us."

A few days later the people did not think
Paul and Barnabas were gods. They didn't like
the things the missionaries were saying. A man
picked up a rock. Soon all the people were
throwing stones at Paul and Barnabas. Paul
was hurt. The mob dragged the bleeding
missionary through the streets to the city
gates. Paul was hit with bigger rocks. The men
who hurt Paul did not believe in Jesus. They
thought the missionary was saying bad things,
and they wanted to kill him. After stoning

Paul, the men walked up to him for a closer look. Paul lay still on the dirt and stones.

"He's dead. Let's go."

But the brave missionary was not dead. As soon as he was able to travel, he kept on his journey. Paul probably walked more than two thousand miles on his missionary trips. Some of the roads he walked on were straight and smooth. Sometimes he climbed steep hills and went down dangerous roads. Paul walked through rain and hot sunshine.

People hurt Paul because he was a believer, but he remained a cheerful and happy person. Paul was a brave hero because he always had faith in God. He gave his best for Jesus. No matter what problems came, Paul the apostle knew that the Lord was in charge. He knew that being good did not mean an easy life.

Paul and his friend Silas made a missionary trip together. When they preached in Philippi, they were arrested. The soldiers lashed them with heavy whips before dragging them to jail. They chained Paul and Silas and threw them into a back dungeon, the place reserved for the worst criminals. Their feet were clamped in stocks.

Paul was hurting all over. The gashes made by the whip were still bleeding. There was no way Paul and Silas could get comfortable. They must have felt like crying.

Instead, the missionaries prayed and sang hymns. In the middle of the night, an earthquake shook the jail. The chains fell off, and the stocks burst open. The men were free! The jailer thought the prisoners had escaped, and he was so frightened he tried to kill

himself. "Stop!" cried Paul. "We're here."
Then Paul told the jailer about Jesus, and the
jailer and his family believed and were saved.

Thinkback: Where was Paul when he healed a
crippled man?
   What did the angry people use when they
tried to kill Paul and Barnabas?
   Who was the missionary that was put into
jail with Paul?

Shipwreck!

Paul had a mission. Nothing could keep him from sharing with others the good news of Jesus Christ. He traveled many miles on this mission. He traveled farther over sea than on land — probably five thousand miles. It was on a trip by sea that Paul showed again what kind of person he was.

Paul was a prisoner on a ship bound for Rome. The winds were whipping the big sails around like scarves. Paul and the other prisoners talked about the danger they were in. Paul knew the ship might crash in the terrible storm. He decided to talk to the ship's officers.

"Sirs," the missionary said, "the storm is getting worse. With these strong winds, the ship might sink. It can't take much more."

But the ship's captain wouldn't listen to the prisoner. Wild rains pounded the deck. The sailors tied the ropes as tightly as they could, but the sails ripped and split. The storm grew worse, and the ship's crew lost all control. The ship was tossed from the top of one wave to

the bottom of the next. The crew threw
supplies overboard, trying to steady
the dizzy ship.

Some of the sailors were crying: "We're going to drown! We can't get through this awful storm!"

Paul remained calm. "Don't worry," he smiled. "We're all going to be saved. I talked to the God that I belong to, and he told me we would be all right."

Just then the ship hit a sand bar. Wild waves crashed against the ship, and it began to fall apart. The boatmen and the prisoners jumped into the water and started swimming.

The men who couldn't swim grabbed boards or broken pieces of the ship and

floated to the beach. Paul splashed through the rough water. He finally touched the sandy bottom and stood up. A sailor who was lying half in the water and half on the sand reached out, and Paul helped him up. Together they struggled up on the beach, glad that they were alive. Just as Paul had said, the boatmen and prisoners were all right.

The people who lived on the island ran to the beach. They built a big bonfire so the wet men could get warm. Missionary Paul bent over and picked up an armful of sticks to throw on the fire. A snake crawled from one of the logs. Before Paul could move, the snake struck him on the arm. A man screamed.

"Oh, he will die!" someone cried.

Everyone waited in fear, expecting Paul to fall dead. But Paul calmly shook off the snake and warmed his hands at the fire.

"Did you see that!" the people said. "This man must be a god. The poison of that snake would have killed anyone else."

Then one of Paul's friends spoke up: "Paul is a Christian leader on the way to Rome. He is a missionary for Jesus Christ. Paul's power comes from the Lord Jesus."

Paul stayed on the island of Malta about three months. He healed sick persons and preached and told everyone he met that Jesus Christ was the Savior.

Thinkback: Why do you think Paul was not afraid when the ship was in the storm?

38

My Best for Jesus

No matter where Paul was — in prison, on a ship, walking across a desert, or at a beach bonfire — he was a man with a mission. He knew his purpose in life, and that was to serve his Lord. When he was a prisoner in Rome, he still set a good example.

Paul was not in jail in Rome, but he was guarded by a soldier. This guard had never met a prisoner like Paul. Never complaining, the prisoner wrote letters, talked with his friends, and asked the guard about his family. Sharing Jesus with the Roman soldier who guarded him was a natural thing for Paul to do.

One visitor the guard noticed was a young runaway slave, Onesimus. This slave, sometimes called "Useless," had run away from his owner, Philemon.

"Useless" was not welcomed by the people of Rome. If he was a runaway, he had probably stolen something, they thought. Nobody liked Onesimus — that is, nobody except Paul. After Paul told Onesimus about Jesus, everything was different.

For one thing, Onesimus was not mad at Philemon any more. He was not afraid. The slave who had run away from his owner wanted forgiveness. Paul wrote a letter to Onesimus' master. Philemon was a Christian — Paul had led him to trust Jesus. The letter said:

"I want to ask a favor of you. Please take Onesimus back — but not as a slave. Welcome him like a brother. Onesimus is now a Christian, and he wants you to forgive him. If he owes you any money, I will pay it."

Paul was not perfect. He was human, and he made mistakes. But he always tried to do the right thing. Paul made friends easily. He was a caring and loving person.

Paul was forgiving, too. When John Mark quit the missionary trip with Paul and Barnabas, Paul was mad at first. He was

disgusted to think that John Mark would start a missionary trip and leave when the going got rough. But Paul forgave him. Later on, Paul wrote a letter to a friend asking him to bring John Mark with him, adding "for he is useful in God's work."

Paul, the writer and preacher, was strong and brave in his travels and adventures for Christ. At the same time he was tender and kind. When his friends bickered and fussed, Paul showed them how to forgive and love one another.

In a letter to Timothy, Paul wrote:

"Be strong, my young friend. Living for Jesus is not easy, but it is the only way. I have had some hard times, but I knew what God wanted me to do.

"I have done my best for Jesus."

Thinkback: How could Paul help people even when he was in prison?

What do you think was the secret of Paul's courage?

Reflections

Do you think you would have liked Paul?
What was Paul's mission?
Do you think Paul was a happy person?

From his own writings, we can tell that Paul was cheerful and good-natured. The mighty leader knew that God was in control of his life. He was not afraid. From prison, Paul wrote in a letter to the Philippians: "Rejoice in the Lord always; again I say, Rejoice."

Paul was a great missionary, a messenger for God. His letters in the New Testament help us to know more about how Jesus wants us to live. You may want to read the book of Acts to learn more about the exciting life of Paul.

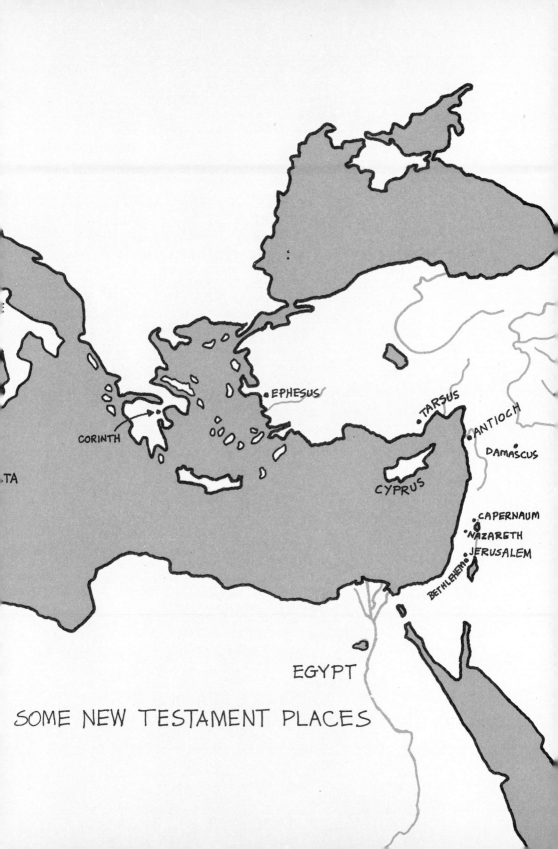

SOME NEW TESTAMENT PLACES